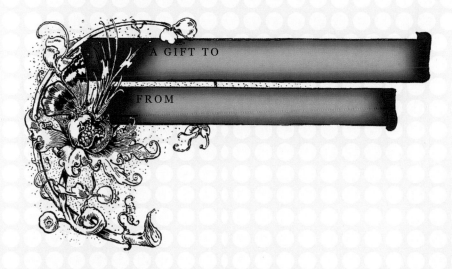

A GIFT TO

FROM

PUBLISHED IN NASHVILLE, TENNESSEE, BY THOMAS NELSON.
THOMAS NELSON IS A REGISTERED TRADEMARK OF THOMAS NELSON, INC.

PROJECT EDITOR: MACKENZIE CLARK HOWARD
ART DIRECTION & DESIGN & FOOD STYLING BY: LINDA BOURDEAUX, THEDESIGNDESK.COM
PRODUCTION BY: GRETCHEN STIBOLT
FRONT COVER & INTERIOR IMAGES EXCEPT FOR PAGES 29, 65, 94, 105, 153, 157,159 © 2008 SCOTT SCHRECKER PHOTOGRAPHY
PHOTO OF BETHANY THOUIN BY ED RODE PHOTOGRAPHY
SPECIAL THANKS TO NINA RETTLER FOR THE USE OF HER BEAUTIFUL HOME.
THANK YOU TO OUR MODELS: KELLY GREENE, DIANA BEACH,
SHACINA BEARD, NICOLETTE SMITH, HOLLY CHAPMAN AND ANNA AVERA
ALL CHOCOLATES EXCEPT ON PAGES 58, 94, 153, 157, 159 BY: BETHANY THOUIN, CHOCOLATIER
IMAGES ON PAGES 29, 65, 94, 153, 157,159 © 2008 SHUTTERSTOCK PHOTOGRAPHY

THOMAS NELSON, INC. TITLES MAY BE PURCHASED IN BULK FOR EDUCATIONAL, BUSINESS, FUND-RAISING, OR SALES
PROMOTIONAL USE. FOR INFORMATION, PLEASE E-MAIL SPECIALMARKETS@THOMASNELSON.COM.

ISBN-10: 1-4041-0525-5
ISBN-13: 978-1-4041-0525-6

PRINTED AND BOUND IN CHINA

WWW.THOMASNELSON.COM

CHOCOLATE COVERED

FRIENDSHIP

ARTISAN CHOCOLATIER BETHANY THOUIN
& ANGELA FOX

THOMAS NELSON
Since 1798

NASHVILLE   DALLAS   MEXICO CITY   RIO DE JANEIRO   BEIJING

FOR Jessie Lyric

May you always have a friend beside you . . .

—Bethany

FOR Jessica

—Angela

Table of Contents

Drama . . . trauma . . . and making chocolate in my pajamas—that about sums up the last few years of my life in a truffle shell. Creating an artisan chocolate business is not all *chocolat* and roses, I assure you (although the movie *Chocolat* still inspires me!).

Through all the professional and personal pain and trials I've experienced, one thing remains constant—the importance of friendship. As I look back, I see in my mind the faces of hundreds of friends who stand at each marker of my journey. Their warm smiles, kind eyes, and encouraging words still sustain me. These friends bring life to my story and meaning to my heartache.

Over the years my friends have been my champions. They have wiped my tears, clothed my children, fed my family, and rubbed my aching shoulders. They have comforted my newborn, and they have held my husband as he cried. Without each act of kindness that they have so graciously extended, I would not be the person I am today. Bethany:Chocolatier, my beloved chocolate business, would still be just a dream.

Because I am so indebted to friendship, I will joyfully and willingly be a friend to those who are hurting, hungry, and broken. I will share with them the treasures that I have been so fortunate to enjoy in the hope that these precious souls will know what it feels like to be loved.

You see, gratitude carves a grand canyon in a heart made tender by pain. The depth can't be adequately described. It is something that has to be experienced. Who can explain how it feels to be handed hope when you were sure your chance had passed? Who can describe what it is like to look into the eyes of the giver and see a glimmer of understanding and not a hint of judgment? That is friendship.

And now I'd like to introduce you to a friend of mine. She's honest and giving, good and true. She's stimulating, inspiring, and, oh, a little bit messy too. As a matter of fact, you might be very well acquainted with her. She is Chocolate.

I often describe chocolate as being a woman. And I want you to know her—her origins, her processes, her temperament, her wisdom—the way that I know her.

Friendship and chocolate are so intertwined for me that I name each and every truffle I create after a friend of mine who shares specific qualities with that truffle. As I introduce you to those friends in this book, I'll also talk about the characteristics of both the chocolate and the friendship that make them a necessary and addictive part of life.

Above all else, as you join in my story, I want you to see the evidence that God designed all these things. He delights in our pleasure. Chocolate is proof enough of that! ❊

CHAPTER ONE

Chocolate Listens

TINA'S DARK CHOCOLATE TRUFFLE
❧ THE ONE YOU ALWAYS COME BACK TO ❧

A BLEND OF TWO OF THE WORLD'S FINEST DARK CHOCOLATES

FLAVOR ACCENTED WITH A SPLASH OF PURE MEXICAN VANILLA

ROLLED IN PURE UNSWEETENED COCOA POWDER

My friend Tina is my quiet secret keeper. I tell her everything that I think and feel, both rational and irrational, and she listens. My trust in her is one of the most valuable gems in my heart. But it wasn't always this way. Friendships are never perfect, but great friends learn and mature from their mistakes; they extend grace instead of settling for division.

Tina and I have been through a lot together. We grew up together, recorded an album together, and moved across the country together. We were married within a few years of each other, we had our first babies together, and we lost our fathers to tragic deaths together.

Together we have also experienced great pain because of a seemingly irrevocable breach of trust. For two years Tina and I didn't speak.

I missed the life-threatening birth of her second child, and she missed the heart-wrenching trials of my divorce. The void was cavernous. I would hold the phone in my hand and weep because I couldn't make myself dial her number. Her husband watched helplessly as she lay on the floor sobbing and pounding her fists into the carpet over our severed friendship.

But the pain was so deep. Time was a necessary element in our healing. So we waited, and as the seasons changed, so did we. At first the pain clung to us like the suffocating humidity of the summer. Then it slowly changed us so that, like the fallen leaves of autumn, we were dried up and thirsty, only to be blown about by a cold, bitter winter wind. When the icy pain finally subsided, spring arrived, and we were able to look in each other's eyes once more. We held each other's children, and together we celebrated these signs of new life budding on the branches of our too-long-latent friendship.

Now those blossomed branches hang over us, giving us sweet shade as we sit together, whispering our secrets and keeping them safe.

Listen carefully to Me, and eat what is good,
And let your soul delight itself in abundance. —*Isaiah 55:2b*

When it came time for me to create a truffle for Tina, I thought long and hard about what to do. Since Tina is my best friend, she needed the best truffle. I went to my favorite organic grocer and walked down the aisles looking for that extra special ingredient that would say, "Tina." I never found it. So then I thought about her favorite flavors, the scents I knew she loved, and the spices that always made her happy, but I still couldn't find the perfect inspiration for "her" truffle. Several days later, as I was enjoying my favorite truffle—a classic dark truffle covered in cocoa powder—I thought about how I always seem to come back to this truffle. Even with all the interesting flavor combinations that are out there, this is the one that comforts me. That is when I realized that I had had Tina's truffle all along. It was the first truffle that I learned how to make—the classic, the basic, the tried and true, the one I always come back to! ❊

And I Stir . . .

My workshop is cold and empty.

I am exhausted and lonely,

But the chocolate needs stirring.

Cruel thoughts lead me down a dark hallway,

Strap me to a hard, wooden chair,

Torture me with pulses of doubt and fear.

I open my eyes and shake my head.

Who will rescue me?

And I stir.

Her sweet smell casts a light into my darkness,

Calling me out.

To my surprise I want to follow.

And I stir.

Thick, fluid chocolate

Charms my captor into letting go,

Allowing a reprieve.

The dark mixture envelops my thoughts.

And I stir.

I slowly feel my senses return

As I reveal my intimate thoughts to her.

And I stir.

And she listens.

Keeping my secrets safe

Giving me a voice

Never judging

Only listening.

And I stir.

And I'm free.

My friend Chocolate is temperamental and very particular about how she should be treated. If you show her love, she will dazzle you with her beauty, but if you leave her unattended, she will be unworkable and barely recognizable as the woman who was so beautiful only a few hours ago.

We women like to think we are easy to handle, but if we're really honest with ourselves, we can admit that learning how to handle us can be a difficult task that takes practice and patience. Likewise, working with chocolate requires a resolve that you will never be right all of the time, nor will you get it right all of the time. There will always be a timing issue or a temperature or climate problem that will complicate things. Don't resent this. Rather, embrace it, for it is part of Chocolate's charm. As long as you remain patient and open, you will find that acceptance and forgiveness are two of her richest qualities. She wants to be tempered, and she longs to be beautiful. She needs to be coerced into the change, but she will give her wholehearted devotion to the chocolatier who masters the tempering technique.

In this delicate relationship, you will find a kind of companionship. As I stand here stirring the chocolate, the aroma that envelops me is captivating and mesmerizing. I get lost in the lovely scent. I contemplate life and relationships, and I stir all of my worries into that bowl of chocolate. When the chocolate is finally tempered, my worries somehow dissipate, and I know that my friend Chocolate will keep them safe.

Just as chocolate becomes beautiful through the process of being tempered, we become beautiful as we let our experiences temper us—and friendship brings us a wealth of those tempering experiences. Every one of us has been hurt by a friend, and sadly, we have all hurt a friend at one time or another. Tina and I have been tried and stretched and tempered, but now that we have come to the other side, our friendship is deeper, richer, and more precious than ever. Learning how to be a friend is a lifelong journey, one that can produce some of life's most satisfying fruit.

"I stir my worries into a bowl of melted chocolate, then lick my fingers, and remember that life is good." —*Crystal Thomas*

Keeping secrets and sharing burdens are two practices of friendship. They're beautiful exercises that require patience and self-control. I'm so grateful for the opportunities to sharpen these skills among and for my friends, and I'm so thankful for Tina (and chocolate!) who keep my secrets and share my burdens. ✷

How to Temper Chocolate

YOU WILL NEED

1 pound of chocolate (milk, dark, or white) chopped into bite-sized pieces, divided

1 microwave-safe bowl

1 rubber spatula

1 digital thermometer

TEMPERING IS THE PROCESS OF MELTING CHOCOLATE and taking it through a series of temperature changes so that its cocoa-butter crystals reach their most stable form. When you melt chocolate, you take it from its tempered state to its untempered state. In order to get the beautiful appearance back, you have to temper the chocolate or, in other words, make it behave. Untempered chocolate will have a matte or filmy surface and will crumble when broken, but proper tempering produces a nice shine and a clean snap.

PLACE ⅔ OF THE POUND OF THE CHOCOLATE in a microwave-safe bowl. Melt the chocolate, stirring at 30-second intervals until the chocolate reaches 115° (110° if you are using white chocolate). After it has reached the desired temperature, remove from microwave and add a small handful of the remaining ⅓ pound of chocolate bits into the melted chocolate and stir constantly. Repeat this step until either all the chocolate has been stirred into the bowl and has melted or the chocolate has reached 89°. At this point the chocolate should be tempered and ready to use for dipping or molding. You can test it by dipping the end of a plastic utensil into the chocolate and letting it rest for two minutes. The chocolate should set up quickly; it should be dry to the touch and have a shiny finish.

CHAPTER TWO

Chocolate Is Honest

BECK'S MARGARITA TRUFFLE
❧ THE ONE THAT MAKES YOU HONEST ❧

WHITE CHOCOLATE INFUSED WITH LIME

A SPLASH OF TEQUILA • DIPPED IN WHITE CHOCOLATE

DROPPED ON SEA SALT • TOPPED WITH LIME ZEST

❧ TELL IT LIKE IT IS ❧

You know the kind of person who will go to a movie all by herself, sit prominently in the center seat, and laugh conspicuously and freely throughout the whole film? Well, that's my gloriously independent friend Becky. The codependent in me is awed by her ability to be with herself and by herself, and be completely okay with that. She knows who she is and what she believes. Even in the face of opposition, she is unwavering in her convictions. She is one of the freest and most honest people I know. She's honest with herself, and she's honest with the people she loves. She has the intrepid ability to tell people the truth!

Becky enjoys being around people who know who they are, and if you don't know who you are, she'll help you find yourself! It is very apparent that Becky values the differing perspectives of her friends; she simply expects anyone who engages in a conversation with her to have a backbone. Every now and then her unadulterated honesty is even hard for me to take, but she's okay with that! In fact, in those moments when I squirm, Becky is usually saying exactly what I need to hear, and I know she's being real with me because she loves me. She doesn't expect me to share all of her opinions, but she does expect me to know what I believe and why I believe it. She has a way of getting through the feelings, fluff, and philosophies to the heart of an issue; she targets the issue in its purest form and takes me with her in the process.

Those qualities in Becky have enabled me to learn a lot about myself.

Just as Becky is not afraid to tell me the truth when I need to hear it, she is equally ready and able to give strong encouragement and affirmation. As I began pursuing my dream of becoming a chocolatier, Becky was like a career coach for me. During those tough first years of business, she didn't lavish me with compliments or tell me what I wanted to hear. Instead, she kept me focused on my dream and constantly reminded me, "This is what you wanted! Don't quit now!" Sometimes after we talked, I'd think, *Wow! I just had a great session with Dr. Phil!*

Let your light so shine before men, that they may see your good works and glorify your Father in heaven. — *Matthew 5:16*

I created the margarita truffle with Becky in mind. The tequila represents her unwavering conviction, the lime is abrasive but sweet, and the salt represents her ability to bring out the flavor in her friends. She is a remarkable woman, and I'm honored to call her a friend. ❋

The Girls Ran Home

The moment of truth stared us all down,
Dared us to run or take to the ground.
I clenched my fists; surprised, I admit,
At the courage I'd found.

The girls ran home.
The girls ran home.
I was the one left standing
When the girls ran home.

When the dust settled I looked around,
And saw one as brave. She dusted me down.
She said, "How does it feel to know that you claimed
The stake in your ground?"

The girls ran home.
The girls ran home.
I was the one left standing
When the girls ran home.

We weren't there long when I noticed around me
The women who'd learned to fight long before me.
We wept as we shared the stories we'd earned
Of the day we learned to survive.

I dare you to come in and pull up a chair.
You might be surprised by all that you hear—
The similar thread in our stories
Of no greater pain and no greater glories.

When the girls ran home,
The girls ran home,
We were the ones left standing
When the girls ran home.

Bethany Thouin

© 2005, used by permission

Have you heard the saying, "You can take the girl out of the South, but you can't take the South out of the girl"? The same principle holds true for cocoa beans. Even when they are harvested, processed, and shipped miles and miles away from their homeland, cocoa beans carry with them the unique flavors of the region where they were grown. Chocolate, like people, has the ability to stay true and honest to its roots.

Some of the larger, mainstream chocolate makers import their cocoa beans from all over the world and then blend them together to create a mild and homogeneous flavor. Many fine chocolate manufacturers, on the other hand, embrace the distinctiveness of the regional flavors. Those regional influences make the different varieties of fine chocolate unique and special.

Just as grapes grown in different regions produce distinctive flavors of wine, the flavor of a cocoa bean depends on the natural makeup of the soil, the growing conditions, and the breed of plant that is cultivated in a particular region. Local harvesting and fermentation practices also affect flavor.

Venezuelan chocolate, for instance, is very earthy with a woody kind of taste that makes it the best chocolate to pair with fruit. Chocolate from Madagascar has a fruity flavor and is more acidic in nature, making it a great match for spices.

Just as chocolate carries with it the history of its place of origin, friends have roots that flavor their personalities and idiosyncrasies. It is important to embrace those differences because these unique perspectives give depth and character to our relationships. If you can't reveal your true self and, at the same time, embrace the true self of each of your friends, friendships will never be more than superficial niceties.

"There's nothing better than a good friend, except a good friend with CHOCOLATE." — *Linda Grayson*

When we share our stories with others, we grow in ways that are unexpected and rewarding. What unique qualities do you have to offer in your friendships? Are you being authentic with your friends? And are you helping each of your friends expose her true self to you? When you're with your friends, bring your whole story with you because that's what makes you, *you*. Honest. Unique. True. Your honesty about who you are just might be the only way people will ever get to experience a delicious flavor from your part of the world! ✽

Girls' Night Out

ONCE A MONTH FOR SEVERAL YEARS, I met with a group of women for a night of great food and great stories. We called our group "The Supper Club." Every month we would meet at one of our homes sans husbands and children and share our recipes and our lives with one another. I would always leave with a fresh perspective on life and a deeper understanding of myself, not because I had a chance to talk about my problems, but because I had a chance to see life through someone else's eyes.

At Supper Club, nothing was off-limits: husbands, children, parents, in-laws, envy, loneliness, triumphs, and losses. If we felt it, we discussed it. Through this experience, I realized that I really am okay. I'm not crazy or hopeless. And I'm not perfect, but neither is anyone else.

Good friends should be transparent enough to let one another see their weaknesses. For some reason, we all feel inadequate. But when we realize that we are all struggling with similar feelings and issues, all of a sudden we aren't so alone. And isn't that what we all need to know . . . that we aren't alone?

CHAPTER THREE

Chocolate Is Messy

CRYSTAL'S CORIANDER COCONUT TRUFFLE
THE ONE THAT WON'T BE KEPT

VENEZUELAN MILK CHOCOLATE

INFUSED WITH CORIANDER

TOPPED WITH FRESHLY GRATED COCONUT

WHAT A BEAUTIFUL MESS!

Four years ago a young girl named Crystal floated into my shop and right into my heart. I immediately hired her as my chocolate assistant because I could tell she was oozing with creative talent.

Over the years I came to think of her as a butterfly: she flutters around and brings her unique beauty to those lucky enough to notice. I have often wished that I could capture her spirit and keep it for myself like a child might capture a lightning bug, but I realize that Crystal can't be kept. She needs to be free and fly, not only for her own happiness but also to allow the world around her to catch a glimpse of her beauty.

But I have to say, I don't know how one little butterfly can make such a big mess. The messes Crystal can make are unrivaled! In a perfect world I would have hired another assistant just to follow Crystal around and clean up after her.

One day as I hung up the phone from taking an order, I looked across the kitchen and couldn't believe my eyes. Crystal was on her knees on top of the worktable reaching down into our fifty-pound temperer. She was up to her elbows in chocolate, and she had smears of chocolate on her face and all over her clothes.

I was trying to find the words to ask her what she was doing when I suddenly heard a popping, sizzling sound coming from the stove. Apparently, Crystal had put a pot of cream on to boil before she decided to take her chocolate bath. She looked up at me with "Help!" and "I'm in so much trouble, aren't I?" written all over her face.

I rushed to the stove and turned the burner off just in time to prevent a visit from the fire department, but not quickly enough to stop a tidal wave of cream from spewing over onto the burner and the floor. I still don't know what she was doing in the chocolate, but I do know that it took us a couple of hours to clean up the mess!

I was lucky enough to have Crystal with me for two years before she flew away to pursue her music. Just after she left, she wrote me a letter saying how grateful she was for the time she worked with me. She shared that she had had a terrible complex about herself, her beauty, and her messes, but through the experience of working with chocolate, she learned that God loves her just the way she is—and that somehow He thinks her messes are beautiful!

Crystal's truffle is the only one in my collection that I didn't create. It is fitting that Crystal made it herself, and it speaks of her immense creativity. Coriander and coconut are a unique blend. To me, the coriander symbolizes the way Crystal calms me, and the coconut scattered on top reminds me of her beautiful messes. I named it Crystal's—the one that won't be kept. ✳

Beautiful Mess

Look at the mess I made.
Isn't it perfect?
There's no way to clean it,
No way to hide it.

I lost my innocence.
Doesn't it figure?
And I was the good girl,
Always the good girl.

Although I'm embarrassed
And the fallout is great,
If I could erase it,
I wouldn't replace it.

'Cause now there's no pressure
To try and be perfect.
I know that You love me
Despite what is in me.

I feel strangely grateful
For all I have been through.
Grace turned my mess into
Such a beautiful mess.

As far as the east is from the west,
So far has He removed our transgressions from us.
— *Psalm 103:12*

MELTS IN YOUR MOUTH
. . . AND EVERYWHERE ELSE

Everyone knows that chocolate is messy. In fact, it's nearly impossible to work with chocolate without leaving a delicious stain on your shirt. For a chef, these stains are especially problematic because we are expected to keep our coats clean. But no matter how hard I try, I just can't seem to keep chocolate off the cuff of my coat, the top of my shoe, or even my face! The chocolate on the back of my hand that came from the side of the bowl gets smeared on my cheek. Yes, it's a vicious cycle.

In awe, I watch my friend Stephané, a master chocolatier from Paris, as his spatula glides through the chocolate, leaving it all neatly contained, telling it where to begin and where to end. Even after a full day of hands-on demonstrations, his coat is still pristine. As he watches his students slosh and drip chocolate, his eyebrows begin to twitch in dismay.

I assisted him at the 2007 World Pastry Forum, and at the end of each day, he would look at my chocolate-stained coat and give me a disapproving smile. I would try to change the subject with some profound statement like "Isn't chocolate just like a woman?" Then, in that charming accent, he would respond with something glorious like "Ah, and sugar is like a young girl!"

Stephané has learned that keeping chocolate contained is a carefully developed skill and practically an art. This skill is even rewarded in competition, and for Stephané, that pristine jacket and workplace is a wonderful manifestation of his diligence. As for the rest of us, I guess we'll just keep licking up our delicious drips.

Chocolate has taught me that messy isn't always bad, and that is especially true in friendship. Visualize a bowl filled with chocolate bits—some white, some milk, and some dark. If the room stays cold, the chocolate bits will remain separated. I could even dump them out of the bowl and sort them into white, milk, and dark piles.

But if I put a little heat under that bowl, the bits will begin to melt and the colors will blend, leaving a beautiful mess of chocolate swirls. If I pour it out, I will still see the white, the milk, and the dark chocolates, but I will not be able to separate them.

I think of my friends as different types of chocolate. The cold that keeps us separate is our fears and insecurities. It takes a lot of courage, but as we bravely let our vulnerabilities show, the warmth of that honesty begins to melt our chocolate shells, allowing our hearts and lives to mingle and our influence to rub off on each other. What a beautiful mess! ❄

"Chocolate makes my tummy giggle." — *Emily, age four, overheard at The Cocoa Tree Chocolate Café*

From Bean to Bar

HARVESTING AND FERMENTING COCOA BEANS is a slow and laborious process. If any part of the process is rushed, the chocolate will become too bitter and shallow.

The process begins with the tree. Native to South and Central America, the cocoa tree is cultivated around the equator and can be found in the Caribbean, Africa, Southeast Asia, and the South Pacific islands of Samoa and New Guinea.

The cocoa tree is a tropical plant that grows only in hot, rainy climates. The delicate young trees require shade and protection from wind, so most are planted under the sheltering branches of banana, plantain, or coconut trees.

It takes five years for the trees to begin bearing fruit. The fruit they bear are called pods, which are shaped like footballs and are so disproportionate in size that they appear to defy gravity as they jut straight out from the trunk and from the tree's thick branches. Each of these pods contains thirty to forty cocoa beans, and it takes about twenty-five of these pods to produce two pounds of cocoa beans.

WHEN THE COCOA PODS ARE CUT OPEN, the cocoa beans, which are covered in a gooey white pulp, are removed from the fruit and placed either in piles or in large, shallow wooden boxes and covered with banana leaves to begin the fermentation process. This stage is critical to developing the beans' distinctive flavor and aroma. Fermentation takes from two to eight days, during which time the sugars in the pulp are converted into acids that change the chemical composition of the beans.

The beans are then dried, cleaned, graded, packed, and shipped for processing. Once they arrive at the processing plant, they are roasted and shelled. The center kernel, called a nib, is extracted, finely ground, and used to make a thick paste called chocolate liquor—the base from which all chocolate products are made.

CHAPTER FOUR

Chocolate Satisfies

RENEE'S CHILI PEPPER TRUFFLE
❧ THE ONE THAT SATISFIES ❧

FRENCH CHOCOLATE CENTER

INFUSED WITH CINNAMON AND ORGANIC CHIPOTLE

ENROBED WITH VENEZUELAN CHOCOLATE

SPRINKLED WITH CHILI PEPPER FLAKES

∼ I NEED ME SOME RENEE! ∽

I showed up in Nashville as a starry-eyed single mom ready to make it big in the music industry. I had no family or friends in the area. Just a notebook filled with song lyrics and a head filled with dreams.

You can imagine my nervousness when, trying to get my songwriting career off the ground, I found myself in the office of a music publisher on Music Row. To my surprise, the woman on the other side of the desk welcomed me like an old friend. I remember sitting in her office listening to one great song after another as she shared her favorite songwriters with me. I sat there drinking in every lyric—from Paul McCartney to Joni Mitchell—as the music surrounded us.

That meeting and subsequent meetings like it are some of my favorite memories. Not because I was sitting on Music Row listening to powerful lyrics with a music publisher, but because this woman took the time to be a friend to me.

I had nobody. I was nobody. But Renee didn't care. She shared her heart, her life, and even her church with me. Renee's friendship has been one of the most influential of my life. I was so impressionable and fragile, and I craved her intrinsic confidence. She took me under her wing at a time when I most needed it; she satisfied a void in a way that has helped shape my character and my career.

Renee supported my music and showed up to hear me sing whether I was at the prestigious Bluebird Café or a hole-in-the-wall coffee shop. And when I decided to become a chocolatier, she was right there with me sampling chocolate from all over the world as we discovered the different flavors chocolate offers. It was in her kitchen that I created my first unique truffle.

We are both moms with young children now, so I don't see her as often as I'd like, but I do often hear a great lyric and think, *I need me some Renee!* At the same time, when she eats great chocolate, she thinks, *I need me some Bethany!*

When I created Renee's truffle, I knew that it had to be a bold, impressive flavor, but I wanted it to be equally smooth and sweet. Chili pepper and milk chocolate seemed like a great combination. The chili pepper reminds me of Renee's tenacity. If she is in the room, you know she is in the room! The milk chocolate is for her sweet, vulnerable side, the one you only get to see when you really look. The combination of the spicy with the sweet is an unforgettable experience, just like Renee. One taste—and you will never be the same. ❋

For most women, chocolate hits the spot; it satisfies a craving that nothing else can. Some say it is a physical or chemical craving; some say it is psychological. I say it doesn't really matter . . . I just need chocolate!

This love affair with chocolate isn't just an American thing either. The craving for chocolate is a universal bond that women around the world share. It is a powerful reminder of how much women are alike no matter what part of the globe they call home.

This fact couldn't have been more evident than it was during my recent encounter with Kajal, a little girl from India. Her love for chocolate bonded us together and won her a place in my heart forever.

Kajal is a five-year-old orphan from India who is blind in both eyes. Her foster mother, Karthi, introduced her to me one morning at the library. I was trying very hard to convince Kajal to say, "Hello" or even acknowledge me, but she would have nothing to do with it!

Despite the cultural barrier, I was determined to connect with this precious child. I knelt down beside her and tried to break through. Even my best attempts failed miserably. Kajal continued to act as if she couldn't hear a thing I was saying—until one powerful word broke the ice . . . chocolate. I couldn't believe it. I'd uttered the magic password! Chocolate had definitely satisfied her on at least one occasion. And now it was my "in" with her.

I went on to tell Kajal that I owned a chocolate workshop where I make chocolate all day long, and she instantly became my new BFF (best friend forever). That one word was all it took. I had her undivided attention as I went on to describe all the different things I can do with chocolate. I promised her that I would let her help me if she visited me in the workshop. I wanted to be the kind of satisfier and void filler for Kajal and Karthi that Renee has always been for me.

> "I have come that they may have life, and that they may have it more abundantly. — *John 10:10b*

Karthi is now living through the heartbreak of an unsuccessful adoption attempt, but she told me that some of her fondest memories of her short time with Kajal were at my chocolate shop, enjoying chocolate in all the different ways that captured Kajal's imagination that day we met in the library.

The bond that they shared, the bond that we shared, even though brief, was rich and unforgettable. Some lifetimes are lived in a few short satisfying moments. Like chocolate, those moments are gone before you know it, but you'll always remember the way they made you feel. ❋

Kajal

You came by surprise
Into my life.
I thought I knew all the pleasures.

Then you filled my senses—
Your voice, your touch, your way.

You captured my imagination
And changed my perspective;
Somehow I knew
I would never be the same.

You left by surprise,
Gone from my life.
I thought I had you and all your pleasures.

But you still fill my senses—
Your voice, your touch, your way.

You captured my imagination
And you changed my perspective;
Thank you, my friend.
I will never be the same.

"The divine drink which builds up resistance and fights fatigue. A cup of this precious drink permits man to walk for a whole day without food."
— *Hernando Cortés, 1519, on drinking chocolate*

Mayan Hot Chocolate

YOU WILL NEED

1 whole dried chili
  pepper

2 cups whole milk

1 cinnamon stick

4 ounces dark
  chocolate, chopped

1 stainless steel bowl

1 saucepan

1 sieve

PLACE CHOPPED CHOCOLATE IN SMALL STAINLESS STEEL BOWL. Set aside. Cut chili pepper open lengthwise. Combine milk, chili pepper, and cinnamon stick in saucepan. Bring just to a boil. Pour milk over the chopped chocolate, using a sieve to keep the chili pepper fragments out of the mixture. Whisk vigorously until chocolate is melted and milk is frothy. Pour into preheated mugs.

CHAPTER FIVE

Chocolate Is Good

LIZ'S MILK CHOCOLATE TRUFFLE
◦ THE ONE EVERYBODY LOVES ◦

BLENDS FRENCH AND VENEZUELAN CHOCOLATE

ACCENTED WITH A SPLASH OF PURE MEXICAN VANILLA

ROLLED IN CHOPPED CHOCOLATE

Liz is my sister-in-law, and she is just plain good. I'm not saying she's perfect, and she'd be the first to confirm that. I simply mean that she is good, as in June-Cleaver-meets-Carol-Brady-meets-Claire-Huxtable good.

Not to overstate my point, but she is a good mom, a good friend, and a good listener. She's good at fixing things, and she's good at making things like curtains and stained glass and wooden shelves. She's even good at installing kitchen sinks!

When I think about why she is this way, the word *intentional* comes to mind. She is so intentional in her decisions and in her efforts that she can't help but succeed. When she commits to doing something, she notices every little detail, and she doesn't quit until she gets it right. I love this about her, even though at times it makes me feel like a complete loser!

With Liz, it isn't a fake good or a shallow reaction to life; it isn't a search for approval or her way of filling a void. I believe it is a pure expression of her very nature—of who God made her to be and who she is content to be. That is what inspires me—Liz's ability to be content with herself.

Her goodness spilled over into my chocolate business, when, very early on in my career as a chocolatier, I had created my first six truffle flavors, and I was ready to show them off to my friends. I hosted a tasting party so I could get their feedback on my new venture. After the party, Liz asked me why I didn't have any milk chocolate truffles.

It hadn't even dawned on me that I'd only used dark chocolate in these six truffles. I had completely missed the fact that some people—including Liz—prefer milk chocolate. So the next day I ordered a very special 41 percent milk chocolate from Venezuela and got busy making Liz's truffle.

Oh, taste and see that the LORD is good;
Blessed is the man who trusts in Him! — *Psalm 34:8*

As I contemplated what flavor I wanted to infuse into her truffle, I thought about how purely good she is. I realized that I didn't want to add anything. The perfect flavor for Liz would be one that would be just pure and plain goodness with nothing added that would distract from the rich milk-chocolate flavor.

To this day, Liz's Milk Chocolate Truffle is one of my best sellers. So, thank you, Liz, for being my first die-hard milk chocolate fan— and for being just plain happy with who you are. ❊

Tasting the smooth, silky, rich flavor of chocolate is a wonderfully self-indulgent experience, one that is treasured throughout the world. Whether it is in a cake, a cookie, or a pie—in coffee, ice cream, or pudding—and even if it's just a morsel, chocolate teaches us that tasting is good. Like chocolate, friendship is rich with goodness. Its sweetness and loveliness are there for the tasting.

Have you ever considered that tasting is a choice?

This concept became very clear to me after my youngest son, Bridge, was born. At eight months he was diagnosed with failure to thrive. (Children who fail to thrive don't receive or are unable to take in, retain, or utilize the calories needed to gain weight and grow as expected.) For over a year thereafter, I watched helplessly as he refused to eat; he literally would not put food in his mouth. We bounced from doctor to doctor, spent weeks in the hospital, and went through surgery and countless medical procedures. I began to wonder if I would even get to see my son grow up. Bridge is now five years old, and even though he still has the feeding port in his tummy, he is eating on his own and growing like a weed! Praise the Lord!

It was during this difficult time that I realized we can look at food and watch others partake, but until we choose to taste, we will not experience the flavors for ourselves.

Like the food that nourishes us, life is meant to be consumed. We need to eat life, consume it conspicuously, and take it fully into our being. How tragic it is to sit on the sidelines of life, letting all the moments pass us by without ever choosing to experience it fully with all of our senses.

"Anything is good if it's made of chocolate."
— *Jo Brand*

Tasting life fully means taking that art class you've always wanted to take but haven't because you feared you lacked talent. It's feeling the joy of a peanut-butter-and-jelly-faced kiss from your child without worrying about getting sticky. It's eating dessert first because you can. It's belting out your favorite tune as you sit at a traffic light despite the neighboring drivers' stares. It is choosing to consume the blessings God has put all around you. And, of course, it's eating chocolate, because God gave it to us richly to enjoy. ✽

Life is an opportunity, benefit from it.

Life is beauty, admire it.

Life is bliss, taste it.

Life is a dream, realize it.

Life is a challenge, meet it.

Life is a duty, complete it.

Life is a game, play it.

Life is a promise, fulfill it.

Life is sorrow, overcome it.

Life is a song, sing it.

Life is a struggle, accept it.

Life is a tragedy, confront it.

Life is an adventure, dare it.

Life is luck, make it.

Life is too precious, do not destroy it.

Life is life, fight for it.

— *Mother Teresa*

How to Purchase Quality Chocolate

1. ASSESS THE COCOA CONTENT: Chocolate is labeled with a percentage of cocoa (or cacao) content. This percentage determines how light or dark the chocolate is, and that information indicates its sweetness or bitterness.

MILK CHOCOLATE usually falls in the 35 to 49 percent range. Milk chocolate generally tastes sweeter because of the amount of sugar added to the cocoa liquor. The milk makes this kind of chocolate irresistibly creamy.

DARK CHOCOLATE (semisweet and bittersweet) will typically fall in the 50 to 80 percent range. Semisweet chocolate, which will be closer to 50 percent and has more sugar, is the sweetest of the darks, so most people prefer its taste. Bittersweet is on the higher end of the range and has less sugar, but it is nevertheless considered the best chocolate for tasting. A cocoa content of 70 percent is optimal—not too sweet, but intense enough to enjoy the flavor of the chocolate.

BITTER CHOCOLATE will contain between 85 and 100 percent cocoa content. Bitter chocolate is the most intense in flavor because it has almost no sugar.

2. READ THE INGREDIENT LIST ON THE LABEL. The only ingredients that should be listed are: cocoa liquor, sugar, cocoa butter, lecithin, and vanilla. The order in which the ingredients are listed is also important. In dark chocolate, cocoa liquor should be listed first. When a dark chocolate bar has sugar listed as the first ingredient, the flavor of the chocolate isn't going to be showcased. Also, watch out for vanillin, which is artificial vanilla. A company that is putting cheap ingredients in their product is not putting out a high-quality chocolate.

CHAPTER SIX

Chocolate Stimulates

KELLY'S COFFEE TRUFFLE
❧ THE ONE THAT KEEPS YOU GOING ☙

AN EXOTIC BLEND OF IMPORTED CHOCOLATE

INFUSED WITH ETHIOPIAN YIRGACHEFFE COFFEE

TOPPED WITH A WHOLE COFFEE BEAN FOR A CRUNCHY BURST OF FLAVOR

My friend Kelly keeps me in stitches with her tall tales—that are actually true!—about her countrified Southern family. This family reads Jeff Foxworthy's *You Might Be a Redneck If* . . . books like they are biographies. In fact, they could be poster children for these books!

One of my favorite stories is about Kelly's grandmother, Nana, who wanted to help her young Vietnamese friend find a good American name for her daughter. She wanted her baby girl to fit in well with her American peers, so Nana advised her friend to name her baby after her granddaughter, Kelly. The problem? The pronunciation of Kelly was lost in Nana's thick country drawl, and the name given to the child was not Kelly, but Killy—spelled and pronounced exactly how Nana said it!

I love how Kelly keeps me laughing and looking on the bright side. Her most valuable contributions to my life are her gifts of verbal affirmation. She is so quick to find the good in a bad situation. Even during the most difficult times in her life, her words to me are encouraging and uplifting as she artfully talks me out of the trees. I can hang up the phone and think, *How did that happen? My house just burned down, and I can't wait to get home and start sweeping up the ashes.*

Like a good cup of coffee, Kelly keeps me going. That's why I created Kelly's Coffee Truffle. Her exuberance for living life to the fullest matches the strong flavor of the Ethiopian Yirgacheffe coffee I infused into the dark chocolate ganache center. Just like Kelly, the dark chocolate in this truffle gives me a swift kick in the pants and says, "Get up and get at 'em!" ❋

> But those who wait on the LORD
>   Shall renew their strength;
>   They shall mount up with wings like eagles,
>   They shall run and not be weary,
>   They shall walk and not faint. — *Isaiah 40:31*

The Value of a Friend

Two are better than one,

Because they have a good reward for their labor.

For if they fall, one will lift up his companion.

But woe to him who is alone when he falls,

For he has no one to help him up.

Again, if two lie down together, they will keep warm;

But how can one be warm alone?

Though one may be overpowered by another, two can withstand him.

And a threefold cord is not quickly broken.

— *Ecclesiastes 4:9–12*

It's almost three o'clock in the afternoon. I have to find some chocolate—and fast! If I were at my workshop, it would be as easy as walking over to one of my chocolate warmers with a spoon. But I'm not at my workshop; I'm at home. And not only am I out of chocolate, but my daughter just woke up early from her nap. Fabulous.

She will now proceed to fuss all afternoon. An afternoon with a fussy baby and no chocolate—not a pretty sight! My mind races as I try to concoct a plan.

Aha! I remember seeing a treat bag in my son's dresser. He must have brought it home from a party and squirreled it away. I dash up the stairs to his room, which is on the third floor. Only intense desperation could get me up there at this time of day. I leap over piles of dirty clothes, trip over the Lego pieces, and pull open the drawer with great expectation.

What?! Starbursts, Sweetarts, and Smarties? What self-respecting woman would fill a treat bag with all fruity candy and without any chocolate? It must have been a dad!

I have to think fast. Do I drag the fussy two-year-old to the neighborhood clubhouse to swipe a couple of Hershey's Kisses out of the receptionist's candy bowl? No, I did that yesterday. Do I drive all the way to my shop for some great chocolate, or do I stop at the corner store for a box of Junior Mints?

Once I had Miss Fussy Pants strapped in her car seat, the answer became clear. What's five extra minutes for great chocolate? I cranked up my Carrie Underwood CD and headed to my workshop for my all-time favorite afternoon snack, a warm brownie cookie.

"I think I've scratched the surface after twenty years of marriage. Women want chocolate and conversation." — *Mel Gibson*

Let me tell you, it's a good thing I give myself a discount!

That's the power of chocolate! And I know I'm not alone in my cravings. I hear from customers (especially women) all the time that, like good friends, chocolate truly keeps us going. I don't think our gender would be as capable as it is without chocolate. I think that when God created the cocoa tree, He was thinking of us! ✳

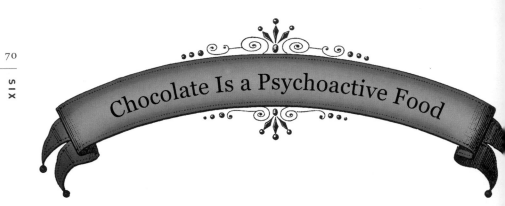

Chocolate Is a Psychoactive Food

MOST WOMEN WOULD AGREE THAT CHOCOLATE CAN SWEETEN a sour mood. It charms us into change. And this effect is not just in our head; science proves it! Chocolate has two chemical ingredients, tryptophan and phenylethylamine, that produce electric messages, or *neurotransmitters*, that tell the brain to behave in a certain way.

TRYPTOPHAN produces the neurotransmitter called serotonin, a common ingredient in antidepressants. Serotonin calms the brain, and high levels of it produce feelings of elation.

PHENYLETHYLAMINE helps the brain release b-endorphin, a hormone generated by the pituitary gland that induces opiate-like responses that decrease pain. This chemical is the reason chocolate has the reputation of being an aphrodisiac. Glorious chocolate actually stimulates the brain's pleasure centers.

As if we needed more excuses to indulge our cravings!

CHAPTER SEVEN

Chocolate Breathes

JULIE ANNA'S ORANGE TRUFFLE
❧ THE ONE THAT REMINDS YOU TO BREATHE ❧

THE DARKEST BLENDS OF CHOCOLATE AVAILABLE

INFUSED WITH FRESH ORANGES AND CLOVES

TOPPED WITH FRESHLY GRATED ORANGE ZEST

One definition of the word *breathe* is "to live; exist." And breathing is, simply, being.

My friend Julie inspires me to just be. Meeting Julie was like taking a deep breath of fresh air on the first day of spring. She is so real. I noticed right away that she was different, but it took me a couple of years to articulate why.

By watching her live life, I learned that Julie is always Julie. She doesn't pretend. If she wants me to go home, she tells me. If she is having a bad day, she explains why she is miserable without complaining.

This attribute makes for a great friendship. I know I can always take Julie at face value. When she appears to be having a good time, she really is having a good time. When she says she wants to go somewhere, she really wants to go. There is no pretense.

This realness makes her very present and generally quite unconcerned about what others may think of her. She has shown me that it is okay to be imperfect, and that frees me to embrace the person I have been becoming over the past thirty-seven years.

I will never forget—and I often recall with a smile—a night when

Julie's five-year-old son came into the living room at bedtime. He was crying because he was scared. A seasoned mother of four, Julie saw through the charade and firmly told him to go to bed.

He stood there and cried even harder, tears and snot flowing down his face, until Julie, who just wanted the liquids to stop streaming, grabbed the closest thing she could find and began wiping his face.

I am not sure what look came across my face at that moment, but whatever it was made Julie stop and notice that she was wiping her precious son's face with . . . underwear. We couldn't help but laugh, and that sent her son over the edge and out of the room with Julie on his heels trying to make it all better.

When she came back into the living room, she didn't try to offer any excuses. She just laughed at herself and joked about her past-due laundry duty. That's exactly what I love about Julie—she's genuine, authentic, and real.

I wanted Julie's truffle to represent her talent for being human, so I made it a little happy and a little dark. The oranges are for her sunny side, and the dark chocolate is for her biting honesty. The nutmeg is the bridge between the two tastes, giving balance to the flavor. I named it Julie Anna's, the one that reminds me to breathe.

The Spirit of God has made me,
And the breath of the Almighty gives me life. — *Job 33:4*

The Purple Song

I want a purple barn with picture windows
So I can laugh when people laugh at me
So I can say as they shake their head
I didn't want to paint it red
I want a purple barn

I want a purple hat with rearview mirrors
So I can laugh when people laugh at me
So I can say I used to care
What everyone thought I should wear
I want a purple hat

I'm bad because I'm bad
No one can make me
I'm glad because I'm glad
No one can make me

I can walk on mountaintops while living on the plains
Or, I can stay and blame it all on you
I choose

I want a purple car with stained glass windows
So I can laugh when people laugh at me
It's funny how we look the same
When looking through a colored pane
I want a purple car

I cry because I cry
No one can make me
I try because I try
No one can make me
I can fly on white wings while walking through the mud
Or, I can fall and blame it all on God
I choose

I want a purple barn with picture windows
So I can laugh when people laugh at me

—*Bethany Thouin*

© 1996, used by permission

It's hard to believe that something as wonderful as chocolate isn't always perfect, but on occasion I have opened a chocolate bar and found a blemished appearance.

You see, Chocolate gets very cranky when she is not stored at the proper temperature. Her surface loses its shine, and a smoky or chalky film called bloom appears. Bloom forms on the surface of the chocolate when the cocoa-butter crystals begin to react to warm temperatures. It isn't harmful, and it doesn't make the chocolate inedible, but it can change the way it feels in your mouth, which affects your perception of its taste.

I find it interesting that the changes happen on the surface. Unlike people, Chocolate does not try to hide her imperfections. I could learn a lesson from her in that department.

If I live my life trying to appear as if I have it all together, I don't allow myself to be fully present in the moment. My children, my husband, and my friends all deserve better than that. I want to give them the best that I have to offer as often as possible.

I don't want to worry about how I'm coming across and what other people think about me. Instead, I want to free my mind and open myself to new thoughts and observations. Rather than being consumed with needless worries, I want to take the time to notice the smell of my baby's hair and to race with my kids across the big green lawn outside our house.

Once we become present with ourselves, we may begin to more readily notice when our friends are feeling or acting less than perfectly. Of course it's not always necessary to point out these moments, but it is important to extend to our friends the same grace that you would like them to offer you when your imperfections surface.

"Strength is the capacity to break a chocolate bar into four pieces with your bare hands—and then eat just one of the pieces." — *Judith Viorst*

Chocolate is perfect and imperfect. If something as wonderful as chocolate can be less than perfect, don't you think you can be too? ✳

Brownie Cookie Recipe

YOU WILL NEED

¼ cup all-purpose flour

¼ teaspoon baking powder

¼ teaspoon salt

7 ounces bittersweet chocolate, chopped

2 tablespoons unsalted butter

2 large eggs

⅔ cup sugar

½ tablespoon strong-brewed coffee

2 teaspoons pure vanilla

½ cup chocolate chips

PREHEAT OVEN TO 350°. Line two baking sheets with parchment paper. In a bowl, whisk together the flour, baking powder, and salt and set aside.

Place the chocolate and the butter in a double boiler. If you don't have a double boiler, you can rig one up by placing a stainless steel bowl on top of a pan of steaming water. Just make sure the bowl doesn't drop all the way into the pan. It should not touch the water below it.

Heat until melted. Remove the chocolate mixture and stir until smooth.

Using an electric mixer, beat the eggs just long enough to break up the yolks. Add the sugar, coffee, and vanilla. Beat on high speed for about 10 minutes until thick.

Fold the chocolate mixture into the egg mixture until partially combined. Add the flour mixture to the batter. Fold in the chocolate chips.

Use an ice cream scoop to drop the batter onto the baking sheets and bake for 16 to 18 minutes. Enjoy!

CHAPTER EIGHT

Chocolate Nourishes

SARAH'S FRANGELICO TRUFFLE
✤ THE ONE THAT MAKES YOU BETTER ✤

VENEZUELAN DARK MILK CHOCOLATE

INFUSED WITH FRANGELICO OR OTHER HAZELNUT LIQUEUR

ROLLED IN TOASTED ORGANIC HAZELNUTS

ɾ THIS MIGHT HURT A LITTLE ɞ

Sarah is my beloved baby sister. She isn't actually a baby anymore. She is a wife and mother of four, but she'll always be my baby sister.

Sarah understands the value of nourishment better than anyone I know. She attended nursing school right out of high school and was a registered nurse with charge-nurse duties by the time she was twenty-one. I admire that, as a nurse, Sarah recognized that the pain she sometimes had to inflict on her patients was truly for their own good. She could administer a shot without remorse because she knew it was making them better.

This skill has translated perfectly into the parenting world. Some people call it tough love; Sarah just calls it "If-you-don't-eat-your-veggies-you-will-sit-there-all-night!" And she means it. Sarah is a wonderful woman and mother, and I aspire to be more like her. Her ability to discipline her children stems from her concern for their well-being—even when it means filling her children's Christmas stockings with crackers and nuts. "Sarah, it's Christmas! Where are the candy canes?"

She doesn't just dispense the discipline pill; she swallows it too. She once went two years without eating sugar. This was especially hard for me to bear because it meant no chocolate. I had created this amazing truffle for her, and she had to wait a year and a half to taste it. Now that's discipline!

Another reason I love Sarah is because she is a constant source of spiritual nourishment. Any encouragement or advice that she gives flows from a carefully tended wellspring of faith. She draws from this place constantly whether she's homeschooling her kids, teaching young girls at church, or taking the time to handwrite letters to me that are chock-full of Scripture.

> [God] gives us richly all things to enjoy.
> — *1 Timothy 6:17b*

I held all of Sarah's wonderful qualities in my heart when I created her truffle. The toasted hazelnuts add nourishment, and the hazelnut liqueur is strong and flavorful. The milk chocolate is for her sweet devotion. I named it Sarah's, the one that makes you better. ✻

Friendship

I was born an empty vessel.

Each friend who came into my life

Poured her spirit into me.

Now I am a vessel,

Full of the beauty of the women

Who have blessed me with their friendship.

My fourth child, Story Valentine, was birthed in a kiddie pool on the second floor of my chocolate shop in the loft apartment where we lived at the time. She arrived at six thirty in the morning, and by ten o'clock her daddy was proudly showing her off to our customers in the shop below.

At just three weeks old, Story began coming to work with me. I wore her against my chest in a sling that my friend Annie had made for me. Story loved it, and so did I. It was wonderful having her with me as I worked with chocolate and greeted my customers. She quickly became our little chocolate mascot as customers and employees passed her around like she was part of their family.

When Story was four months old, she had her first taste of something other than milk—and you'll never guess what it was! Yes, dark chocolate! I noticed one day that she was watching intently as I stirred a huge bowl of chocolate. I wondered if she was beginning to connect that familiar and wonderful smell with the glorious dark liquid that was in front of her.

So I decided to introduce her to the most amazing taste in the world.

After all, could there be a better first food than chocolate? I swirled some chocolate on my finger and put it up to her mouth. Her eyes were wide with excitement as she grabbed my finger and pulled it toward her mouth as if, in her mind, the moment was long overdue.

When the chocolate reached her tongue, the biggest grin came across her face, and she licked every bit of the taste from my finger. It was precious—easily one of my all-time favorite mommy moments. But then she wanted more . . . and more . . . and more. And that has been the story of her life thus far: Story always wants chocolate.

"At no other time has nature concentrated such a wealth of valuable nourishment into such a small space as in the cocoa bean." — *Alexander von Humboldt, nineteenth-century South American natural scientist*

You can imagine my relief as the news media began churning out reports on the healthful qualities of dark chocolate. I've been amazed to watch over the last few years as doctors and researchers verify the health benefits it offers.

Don't get me wrong! I'm certainly not proposing replacing breast milk or formula with chocolate. Heaven forbid! However, reports show that dark chocolate is a potent antioxidant that gobbles up free radicals and destructive molecules that are implicated in heart disease. Chocolate also increases our HDL (good cholesterol) levels the way the omega-3 in salmon does, and *The Journal of the American Medical Association* reported that chocolate can help lower high blood pressure. Plus, the calcium contained in chocolate may actually strengthen tooth enamel.

So I guess I don't have to feel guilty about giving Story chocolate (in moderation, of course) because it's apparently strengthening her teeth, lowering her blood pressure, preventing heart disease, fighting free radicals, increasing good cholesterol, and keeping her in a good mood! Wow, I'm a great mom! ✿

Sarah's Truffle Recipe

YOU WILL NEED

11	ounces milk chocolate
⅓	cup heavy cream
2	tablespoons butter, softened
2	tablespoons Frangelico
1	pound milk chocolate for tempering
¼	cup finely chopped toasted hazelnuts

TO CREATE THE GANACHE, the truffle filling, Stir constantly as you melt the chocolate in a double boiler. Be sure that the chocolate does not go over 110°. When it is completely melted, pull it off the steam and set it aside. In a separate pot, bring the cream just to a boil over medium heat so as not to scorch the cream. Pour the heated cream into the chocolate and stir vigorously until the mixture is smooth. Add the softened butter and stir until melted. Stir in the Frangelico until smooth.

Refrigerate the ganache until it has the consistency of pudding. This should take at least 20 minutes. Then beat the ganache with a hand mixer for 15 seconds. Let the ganache rest until it reaches room temperature.

The ganache should now be firm. Scoop the ganache onto parchment paper using a small ice cream scoop. With the palms of your hands, gently roll the scooped ganache into perfectly round balls. You now have the centers for your truffles, and you are ready to dip them.

Temper 1 pound of chocolate (see directions on pages 18 and 19).

Generously cover the palms of both of your hands with tempered chocolate. Pick up a ganache center and roll it in the palm of your hands until it is thoroughly coated. Set on parchment paper; continue until all centers have been coated. When the first coat is hardened, coat your palms with tempered chocolate again and cover truffles with a second coat. Sprinkle the top with toasted hazelnuts before the chocolate hardens. The wet chocolate will act as glue for the nuts.

"Dad is Great! He Gives Us Chocolate Cake!"

DO YOU REMEMBER BILL COSBY'S HILARIOUS STAND-UP ROUTINE when he talks about—at his wife's command—getting out of bed to go make breakfast for their children? His four-year-old suggested the chocolate cake sitting on the counter. Seeing it as his way out of cooking, Bill considered the ingredients and said, "Eggs, milk, wheat—that's nutrition."

When his wife entered the kitchen, the children were singing in unison, "Dad is great! He gives us chocolate cake!" Needless to say, she was not very happy.

But you know what? In his listing of the benefits of cake for breakfast, ol' Bill missed the most nutritious ingredient of them all— the chocolate!

Did you know?

- A chocolate bar contains more calcium, protein, and vitamin B_2 than a banana or an orange.

- Chocolate contains calcium and fluoride that strengthen teeth and fight cavities.

- During World War II American soldiers were given three chocolate bars as part of their daily ration. This important source of energy could be easily consumed during combat, and it has been used by American forces ever since.

- Chocolate contains theobromine, a chemical with similar effects as caffeine. Theobromine is a bitter alkaloid that is mildly stimulating and diuretic. Because of its ability to dilate blood vessels, it is also used to treat high blood pressure.

Beware, however, if you have pets. Cocoa and chocolate products may be toxic or lethal to dogs because they metabolize theobromine more slowly than we humans do. Fine dark chocolate with a high cocoa content is the most dangerous. A three-and-a-half-ounce dark chocolate bar can be enough to poison a small dog.

CHAPTER NINE

Chocolate Inspires

SOFIA'S SWEET POTATO TRUFFLE

THE ONE THAT INSPIRES

A SMOOTH MILK CHOCOLATE GANACHE

SWEET POTATOES BAKED IN THE SOUTHERN TRADITION
WITH BUTTER, CINNAMON, AND NUTMEG

TOPPED WITH DRIED SWEET POTATO CURL

Oprah Winfrey is a friend I have not yet met. That might sound funny, but just as some people felt a personal closeness and bond with Jacqueline Kennedy Onassis or Princess Diana, for me, it's Oprah. Maybe someone you don't know personally has inspired you. Maybe, like me, you also feel that if you just had the chance to meet this friend, you would be great comrades.

Whether that person is a servant like Mother Teresa, an overcomer like Joni Eareckson Tada, or a courageous reformer like Rosa Parks, women who have done ordinary things through the years have made an extraordinary impact on humanity. In doing so, they touch our lives in ways that inspire us like a close friend does. Although you may never sit on the world's stage, your life and your actions can also inspire the people around you and sometimes even people you'll never meet.

Because of the impact that Oprah, my yet-to-have-met friend, has had on my life, I wanted to do something special for her. On one of her shows, I witnessed the rapture on Oprah's face when she tasted a sweet potato dish. As I watched, I had what she would call an "aha! moment." So, in honor of my friend and her Southern heritage, I went to the grocery store and loaded up on fresh sweet potatoes, *real* butter, heavy cream, nutmeg, brown sugar, and cinnamon. I baked those sweet potatoes in the Southern tradition, pressed them through a sieve, and mixed them into the finest Venezuelan milk chocolate. Then I named it Sofia's Sweet Potato, "the truffle that inspires," after Sofia, the beloved character Oprah brought to life in the movie *The Color Purple*.

> And whatever you do in word or deed, do all in the name of the Lord Jesus, giving thanks to God the Father through Him.
> — *Colossians 3:17*

Sofia's Sweet Potato Truffle has become one of my signature flavors, and until now, no one knew that I created it for Oprah! I hope that someday she will be able to taste my gift and feel the love and admiration that I have for her. Maybe when she does, she will know that she inspired me to be a little stronger and stand a little taller. ❉

Friendship

Friendship needs no studied phrases,
Polished face, or winning wiles;
Friendship deals no lavish praises,
Friendship dons no surface smile.

Friendship follows nature's diction,
Shuns the blandishments of Art,
Boldly severs truth from fiction,
Speaks the language of the heart.

Friendship favors no condition,
Scorns a narrow-minded creed,
Lovingly fulfills its mission,
Be it word or be it deed.

Friendship cheers the faint and weary,
Makes the timid spirit brave,
Warns the erring, lights the dreary,
Smooths the passage to the grave.

Friendship—pure, unselfish friendship—
All through life's allotted span,
Nurtures, strengthens, widens, lengthens
Man's relationship with man.

— Anonymous

I remember when I was invited to present a dress in the New York City Chocolate Show. A *dress*? Yes, you read it right. The annual chocolate show features haute couture dresses and accessories made from chocolate. I'd done a lot of things with chocolate, but making an article of clothing was not one of them!

It seems the more I experience life, the more I realize how insane I really am. I mean, who goes to New York City to appear in front of the world's chocolate industry to try to pull off a chocolate dress— and does so with no kitchen, no reputation, and no practice?

Well, I'd gotten myself into it, so there I was, a week before the event, pouring out slab after slab of tempered chocolate. My assistant Brandon and I then cut them into one thousand perfectly sized panels that would artfully swing from the chocolate dress adorning the willowy figure of a high-fashion model in this prestigious show. No pressure!

When we were sweating through the prepping phase for this huge event, I experienced my favorite part of the day: pulling back the acetate sheets and seeing the beautiful shine on those glorious chocolate squares. It was a nerve-racking experience. Would we finish the three boxes of chocolate panels in time? Would the package hold up as we transported them to New York City? And, most of all, please, dear Lord, don't let that airplane be hot!

The show ended up being a thrilling success. As I watched our model sashaying down the runway, our delicious creation swinging and shimmering under the lights, I thought, *This is an inspiring moment!* To dare to dream so big, to work through our plan so carefully, to carry all our eggs in one basket, and to watch it all come together like a jigsaw puzzle—this was quite an amazing experience. No one can deny that consuming chocolate is an inspiring experience, but that moment at the New York City runway proved to me that chocolate can also be an art form.

And God was very real and very present throughout that experience. He was writing the story as I eagerly turned the pages. It was beautiful to feel Him move through me as I laid out the chocolate tiles in a spectacular random mosaic, as art unfolded in front of my eyes. I will never be the same.

"I have this theory that chocolate slows down the aging process … It may not be true, but do I dare take the chance?" — *Unknown*

How is it that a thought can grow into a vision that can be expressed through a particular medium and shared with the world? How is it that the world can be impacted by an artist's creation in a way that brings growth and change? How is it that I have been given the opportunity to bring a vision like this forward?

The world is bursting with beauty that begs to be interpreted artistically. As a chocolatier, I use chocolate as my medium. Others use paint, clay, words, or music. Whatever medium we choose, let's dare to tell the beautiful story that lives around us to our children, in our neighborhoods, and on the street. Joseph Campbell said, "What we lack are not scientists but poets and people to reveal to the heart what the heart is ready to receive."

If you haven't found your medium for telling the beautiful stories around you, it's time to wake up and smell the chocolate! Dare to create! ✻

Liz's Milk Chocolate Truffle

YOU WILL NEED

- 10 ounces milk chocolate
- ½ cup heavy cream
- 2 teaspoons Mexican vanilla
- ¼ cup finely chopped milk chocolate
- 1 pound milk chocolate (for dipping truffles)

MELT 10 OUNCES OF MILK CHOCOLATE in a double boiler, stirring constantly. Be sure that the chocolate does not go over 110°. When it is completely melted, pull it off the steam and set it aside. In a separate pot, bring the cream just to a boil over medium heat so as not to scorch the cream. Pour the heated cream into the chocolate and stir vigorously until the mixture is smooth. Stir in the Mexican vanilla until smooth.

Refrigerate the ganache until it has the consistency of pudding. This should take at least 20 minutes. Then beat the ganache with a hand mixer for 15 seconds. Let the ganache rest until it reaches room temperature.

The ganache should now be firm. Scoop the ganache onto parchment paper using a small ice cream scoop. With the palms of your hands, gently roll the scooped ganache into perfectly round balls. You now have the centers for your truffles and you are ready to dip them.

Temper 1 pound of milk chocolate (see directions on pages 18 and 19).

Generously cover the palms of both of your hands with tempered chocolate. Pick up a ganache center and roll it in the palm of your hands until it is thoroughly coated. Set on parchment paper; continue until all centers have been coated. When the first coat is hardened, coat your palms with tempered chocolate again and cover truffles with a second coat. Sprinkle the top with finely chopped milk chocolate before the chocolate hardens. The wet chocolate will act as glue for the chopped chocolate.

CHAPTER TEN

Chocolate Pours

KARIN'S IRISH CREAM TRUFFLE
～ THE ONE THAT SOOTHES ～

DARK CHOCOLATE GANACHE CENTER

INFUSED WITH IRISH CREAM • DIPPED IN MILK CHOCOLATE

SPRINKLED WITH CHOPPED WHITE CHOCOLATE

Pouring—the selfless giving of one soul to another—is an important part of any friendship. My friend Karin is my faithful pourer.

I remember being by Karin's side in the delivery room as we anxiously awaited the arrival of her first child. As she lay there breathlessly trying to practice everything she'd learned in her childbirth classes, almost fully dilated and right in the middle of a contraction, she looked over to her husband and said, "Honey, I packed a sandwich for you just in case you get hungry." *What?* I thought. *She packed a sandwich for her husband?* I could just see her in the kitchen, in early labor, getting out the bread and mayonnaise so that he didn't go without a meal while she was having their baby! What a saint!

That's just who Karin is: she's forever pouring herself into her relationships. She has taught me so much about happy little sacrifices. She's shown me the importance of taking a meal to a new mom (even if it's not exactly homemade) and of sitting on the floor to read books to my children despite the busyness of the day. That sacrificial act might not be the thing I most want to do, but the rewards are long lasting. Karin has taught me these lessons not only with her words but also with her actions. She is a woman of beautiful character, and she possesses a quiet strength that keeps her going.

Eventually, with all that pouring, wouldn't one's well run dry? Absolutely. So there should be a constant ebb and flow of pouring and drinking in our relationships. Just as the tides flow back and forth, so should the giving and taking in our friendships.

In addition to showing me the importance of healthy, balanced, give-and-take relationships, another lesson Karin, my faithful pourer, has taught me, is that it is okay to have "me time." In fact, not only is it okay, but it is necessary! It is impossible to give with a happy heart if we haven't taken the time to let God fill us. We need His anointing regularly, and we need the occasional pampering session when we allow ourselves to indulge in our favorite treats!

> Trust in Him at all times, you people;
> Pour out your heart before Him;
> God *is* a refuge for us. Selah — *Psalm 62:8*

In honor of Karin and her favorite flavor, Irish Cream, I created this truffle. She so willingly gives of herself to others, yet she also recognizes the importance of replenishing her soul through strategic time for herself. I dip this truffle in milk chocolate for Karin's sweetness, but the center is a dark chocolate ganache. Just like Karin, it's sweet on the outside and pure and strong on the inside. ✸

She Pours

I am empty:
I need encouragement.
I am lonely:
I need companionship.
I am hungry:
I need nourishment.
She pours.

I am crazy:
I need sanity.
I am guilty:
I need forgiveness.
I am wayward:
I need direction.
She pours.

I am frantic:
I need assurance.
I am angry:
I need humility.
I am weary:
I need endurance.
She pours.

I am thirsty:
I need hydration.
I am fragile:
I need stability.
I am frightened:
I need dignity.

She pours.

I am filled . . .

She needs me,
And I pour.

I fill the fifty-pound melter with dark chocolate chunks, turn on the timer, and turn off the lights. It is time to go home and kiss my children. In the morning I will come back to find the chocolate completely melted and at the perfect temperature to begin the tempering process.

All the work of melting the chocolate is done while I sleep. It's like magic! As I drive to my workshop the next morning, I think about the smell of the warm chocolate that will greet me when I open the door.

This is my favorite part of the day. I reach for a twelve-quart stainless steel bowl and my favorite red spatula, and I know that I am just seconds away from pure bliss. Holding the bowl ready beneath the spout, I feel my pulse quicken as I slowly lift the lever. My precious machine releases over two gallons of warm, sumptuous dark chocolate!

What a sight! The luscious, thick fluid doesn't hesitate as it pours itself so freely from the melter. I can hardly contain myself as I wait for the last drop. Now I can stir and let my mind wander as I enjoy the sight and smell of this rich and beautiful liquid.

It would be very easy for me to take this simple process for granted. What if I lifted the spout and nothing came out? Or what if I had to force the chocolate out with my spatula in big, chunky clumps? I remember a time when I filled the melter but forgot to turn it on before I left for the evening. The next day, when I lifted the lever, there was no warm chocolate, only the same hard chunks I'd left the night before. What a disappointment.

I've noticed that whenever tempered chocolate is poured from one bowl to another, it gives itself completely to the other vessel. Without reservation, Chocolate willingly and beautifully pours herself out. In the same way, I want to pour myself into my friendships. My natural tendency is to hold some of myself back, but when I am emotionally well, when I am tempered, I can pour myself, like chocolate, into the vessel of friendships. When I am tempered, I can stop in the middle of a busy day if someone is in need, and I can simply pour.

I so enjoy it when my friends pour themselves into me. It is satisfying and beautiful. It is affirming and exhilarating. And it is important for us to remember that such friendships must be tended if they are going to continue to pour freely.

If you take a generously giving friend for granted, one day you may lift the lever and find that nothing is left. So take the time to care for your friend's needs. Find opportunities to encourage her. Show her your gratitude for her friendship in creative ways. Lend her a hand even when she doesn't ask. Simply pour yourself into her life the way she pours into yours. ❀

Tips for Handling and Packaging Chocolate

SINCE OUR FRIEND CHOCOLATE CAN BE A FICKLE GAL, it is important to handle her with care. Here are a few tips for handling and packaging finished truffles:

• Truffles may be stored for two weeks when kept at room temperature.

• To prevent fingerprints from blemishing Chocolate's complexion, use disposable food-safe gloves when you handle finished chocolates. If gloves are not available, work quickly so that the warmth of your fingertips does not leave a print.

• If you find that your hands are too warm, use ice cubes to cool them down. Be sure to dry them thoroughly before returning to the chocolate.

- Chocolate that is handled too often will lose its shine. Be sure to decide on your intentions for the chocolate before handling it and then leave it alone. Keep the chocolates separated with paper wrappers so they don't rub against each other, because that also creates blemishes.

- Always work with chocolate in a cool room. The temperature should be no higher than 70°.

- You can extend the shelf life of your truffles by storing them in an airtight container in the refrigerator. Just make sure to bring the container to room temperature after you remove it from the refrigerator. If you open it too soon, the chocolate might bloom.

- When packaging chocolates in cellophane bags, make sure you keep one hand clean to handle the bag and only use the other hand to handle the chocolate. This is a good way to prevent smudges.

- When placing chocolates in a decorative box, cushion the truffles with a piece of gently crinkled parchment paper. You can also fold the paper over the truffles before you close the box to ensure that they don't shuffle around inside the box.

- Always tie your box or cellophane bag with a ribbon. Simple grosgrain is a nice touch. A gift of chocolate that is beautifully presented will make the recipient feel special, loved, and appreciated.

CHAPTER ELEVEN

Chocolate Covers

DANYALLE'S PUMPKIN SPICE TRUFFLE
❧ THE ONE THAT TAKES YOU HOME ❧

BELGIAN CHOCOLATE

JAMAICAN NUTMEG • PUREED ORGANIC PUMPKIN

ROLLED IN CHOPPED PECANS

I vividly remember the scene. I was fourteen years old, sitting in the living room of my childhood home, when my sixteen-year-old sister, Danyalle, began screaming to someone in the backyard.

I ran to the backdoor and watched through the window as my sister stomped her eyeglasses into smithereens on the concrete patio while she loudly petitioned God to heal her terrible eyesight. As my parents and I stood there watching, I learned two things about my sister: she believed with all of her heart that God could do what she asked, and she wasn't afraid of the consequences that her faithful exercise might bring.

But I was terrified! Surely Mom was going to ground her for a year! Those glasses were expensive, and we were not rich. God didn't heal my sister's eyesight, but He was faithful, and He showed all of us just how beautiful Danyalle was—even with her thick glasses. And although my parents were visibly upset by Danyelle's costly demonstration, they took it as an opportunity to share with her their trust in God's sovereignty.

Now, twenty years later, as I look back at that incident, I admire Danyalle for how she has changed and for how she has remained the same. She now wears contacts, but she continues to diligently and passionately petition the Lord for her needs and the needs of those she loves. I am so blessed by my sister's friendship: every day I feel the effects of her faithful prayer covering my life. She covers me just like chocolate covers a strawberry!

And that's what friends do. Friends cover. They intercede. A friend doesn't just say she will pray for you and then get busy with life; she actually takes the time to sit down, meditate on Scripture, and cover her friend in prayer. Our words to God and our words to one another are so important; they can bless or they can curse. When we cover our friends with blessings, we will see the blemishes of the relationship fade and the beauty grow.

> And above all things have fervent love for one another, for "love will cover a multitude of sins." — *1 Peter 4:8*

Danyalle's truffle is Pumpkin Spice, and this signature flavor was an easy choice. When I began thinking about what foods Danyalle loves, I remembered how picky an eater she was when we were young. She didn't like very many things, but one thing she did love was pumpkin pie. I thought this would be a perfect flavor for her, not only because it is one of her favorites, but because when I close my eyes and imagine a pumpkin pie baking, my memory takes me to the lovely smell of home. And that is exactly what Danyalle does for me: she covers me and takes me home. ❈

You're Covered

Like a grassy hill, like snowy ground,
Not even a sound,
You're covered.

Like land stretched beneath a sky full of clouds,
there isn't a doubt,
You're covered.

Like strawberries dipped in chocolate fondue,
and marshmallows, too,
You're covered.

Like children asleep, tucked safe in their bed,
their prayers overhead,
You're covered.

Like shame held beneath a bottomless sea,
never to breathe,
You're covered.

Like sin underneath the innocent blood of
God's only Son . . .
My child,

You're covered.

Chocolate's viscosity, or thickness, is one reason it is so satisfying. It's why chocolate hugs your fingertip when you pull it through a bowl of warm chocolate. And it's what makes fondue so fun. I love dipping strawberries and marshmallows into chocolate's flowing goodness and watching as a new confection is created. I like to think of this process as *covering*.

When chocolate covers, it clings. It isn't like a blanket that can easily be pulled off. When something is covered in chocolate, that something is never the same again. It can't go back to its uncovered state. You can't lick off all the chocolate. You just have to eat it!

Chocolate covers so completely with such a thick, even coat that it can make a blemished strawberry suddenly look perfect. That is exactly the kind of friend that I want to be. I want to be a warm, enveloping blanket of chocolate that will cover my friends and make them beautiful.

I'm so grateful for Danyalle and the friends like her whom God has put into my life, friends who graciously and diligently cover me.

I had been trying to write this book for over two years, but the task was so consuming and daunting. At times I considered abandoning the whole idea. Then, one day, I was having coffee with my good friend Angela, and she asked how the book was coming. I told her how difficult it had been, that I was struggling with feelings of inadequacy, and that my life circumstances were blocking my creative flow. At first, I had a difficult time saying this to Angela, because she is a dedicated and talented writer. But Angela talked me through my feelings and offered her help. Needless to say, she is the reason this book made it to print! More than that, though, she took the time to cover me when I felt vulnerable, a true act of friendship that ended with a great reward for both of us! ✳

Las cosas claras y el chocolate espeso. (Ideas should be clear and chocolate thick.) — *Spanish proverb*

Chocolate Fondue

YOU WILL NEED

1 pound good quality
   dark chocolate

1¼ cup heavy cream

½ cup whole milk

2 teaspoons pure vanilla

CHOCOLATE FONDUE IS ONE OF THE EASIEST, yet most divine chocolate treats you can make. You don't need to rely on chocolate fondue products that you find in grocery or specialty stores because it's simple enough to prepare in your own kitchen. Try this recipe to build your chocolate confidence and see just how easy it is to be a home chocolatier.

Melt chocolate in a double boiler. Bring cream and milk to a boil in a separate pot over medium heat. As soon as the cream and milk begin to boil, slowly pour the mixture into the melted chocolate as you whisk vigorously. When the concoction becomes smooth, stir in the vanilla. Serve warm.

Let your imagination run wild as you plan what to serve with your chocolate fondue. Fruit, nuts, cheese, and even some vegetables are actually very good. Here are a few of my favorite things to dip into chocolate fondue:

Strawberries, Bananas, Green apples, Pears

Marshmallows, Walnuts

Swiss cheese, Red bell peppers (my very favorite!)

CHAPTER TWELVE

Chocolate Sticks

SHANNON'S PEPPERMINT TRUFFLE

❧ THE ONE THAT BRINGS BACK SWEET MEMORIES ❧

INFUSED WITH OIL OF PEPPERMINT

DIPPED IN DARK CHOCOLATE

DUSTED WITH OLD-FASHIONED PEPPERMINT-STICK POWDER

A CHICK, A HICK, AND A PEPPERMINT STICK

Typical ninth-grade high jinks brought my friend Shannon and me together. You know the drill: boy meets girl, boy dates girl, boy dumps girl for different girl. Repeat. Shannon was the newly heartbroken; I was said boy's next girl. Even though we met under those very awkward circumstances, Shannon and I became fast friends—and our friendship has outlasted that boyfriend by twenty-three years.

Shannon and I have never lived in the same town. So in high school we would convince one of our moms to drive us to the other's house for weekend sleepovers. During one of those sleepovers while I was a senior in high school, I found out just how close Shannon would stick in my time of need.

I will preface this story by saying that Shannon and I were both good girls. We rarely did anything we weren't supposed to do, but on this particular night we broke the rules. Just a little.

I had a boyfriend who lived in the same town as Shannon. It was against the rules for me to spend time alone with him, so he and I would often double-date with Shannon and her boyfriend.

This particular weekend I was seeing my boyfriend off to college. By Sunday evening we were really feeling the weight of the good-bye and just wanted to be alone for a while. Shannon offered to cover for us so that we could take a walk in the park—alone.

We were so rarely alone that we didn't know what to do with ourselves. For a while, we sat on a big rock and dreamed about our future together, but then the conversation strayed into a silly discussion about, of all things, hickeys!

A man who has friends must himself be friendly,
But there is a friend who sticks closer than a brother.
— *Proverbs 18:24*

I admitted to him that I had never had a hickey, and he confessed that he didn't even know how to give one. So, stupidly, I pulled up my hair and offered him his first chance. He strategically went for the back of my neck just in case he left a mark.

I knew I was in trouble when he looked at his results and gasped. I was so upset that I left my boyfriend and headed straight to Shannon's house for help.

At this point, I had not seen the damage, but when Shannon let out her own gasp, my heart sank. I knew I was not going to get out of this alive. She yanked me into the bathroom and began experimenting with different colors of foundation and powder in an attempt to hide the infraction. Nothing worked. The mark was too dark. We realized we needed a serious plan.

So Shannon decided to guard me until the hickey disappeared. She promised to make sure I didn't toss my hair the wrong way and, most importantly, to guarantee that no parent got behind me long enough to notice.

Luckily, the plan actually worked. Shannon stuck by my side, repositioning my hair and literally watching my back until the blemish was only a silly memory.

Shannon's truffle is a tribute to our long-lasting friendship. The peppermint is for her Christmas Day birthday—and because old-fashioned peppermint sticks always bring back good memories, just like Shannon does. ✳

Song of the Open Road

[Dear friend,] I give you my hand!
I give you my love more precious than money,
I give you myself before preaching or law;
Will you give me yourself, will you come travel with me?
Shall we stick by each other as long as we live?

— *Walt Whitman*

Tempered chocolate can act like glue, which makes it a great artistic medium. In fact, this ability to act like glue is the reason why those magnificent chocolate showpieces hold together. Attaching a chocolate rose to the toe of a molded chocolate shoe is as easy as dabbing some tempered chocolate on the rose and holding it in place until it dries.

Even cooler, though, is a secret product we chocolatiers use called cold spray. It is an aerosol can that sprays incredibly cold air in order to speed up the drying time of the chocolate glue. The cold air quickly drops the temperature of the chocolate, which causes it to harden and adhere faster.

My most dramatic example of chocolate sticking occurred during the last five seconds of my appearance on the *Food Network Challenge*. I had eight hours to construct a four-foot-tall Statue of Liberty, and time was running out. As a matter of fact, the crowd was counting down, "Ten . . . nine . . . eight . . ." and I had yet to attach Lady Liberty's torch. Just five seconds were left before I had to throw my hands up in the air to signal my finish. I glued the torch to her arm and silently prayed, *Lord, please let this stick!* I didn't want the beautiful torch to come crashing down on national television. Thanks to God and a handy can of cold spray, the torch stuck!

In friendship it is also important to stick. A good friend is one who lives with you through the bad times as well as the good ones and who stays by your side when no one else will.

Chocolate has taught me that, to really stick, you have to apply yourself to the relationship. Not just any part of yourself, but your tempered parts. The parts of you that exemplify the fruits of the Spirit—love, joy, peace, patience, kindness, goodness, faithfulness, gentleness, and self-control. Because, just as untempered chocolate does not have what it takes to stick, untempered relationships will not stick either.

There's no magic can of cold spray in friendship, and the sticking process may be daunting. That process sometimes requires long-suffering, but the reward is great. If we allow our life experiences to temper us, we will have what it takes to stick, and these mature friendships will stick for a lifetime. ❋

"There are four basic food groups: milk chocolate, dark chocolate, white chocolate, and chocolate truffles." — *Unknown*

Shannon's Peppermint Truffle

YOU WILL NEED

- 8 ounces dark chocolate
- ½ cup heavy cream
- 2 teaspoons peppermint extract
- 1 pound dark chocolate for tempering
- ¼ cup finely chopped peppermint sticks

MELT THE CHOCOLATE in a double boiler, stirring constantly. Be sure that the chocolate does not get hotter than 110°. When it is completely melted, pull it off the steam and set it aside. In a separate pot, bring the cream just to a boil over medium heat. Pour the heated cream into the chocolate and stir vigorously until the mixture is smooth. Stir in the peppermint extract.

Refrigerate the ganache until is it has the consistency of pudding. This should take at least 20 minutes. Then beat the ganache with a hand mixer for 15 seconds. Let the ganache rest until it reaches room temperature.

The ganache should now be firm. Scoop the ganache onto parchment paper using a small ice cream scoop. With the palms of your hands, gently roll the scooped ganache into perfectly round balls. You now have the centers for your truffles and you are ready to dip them.

Temper 1 pound of chocolate (see directions on pages 18 and 19).

Generously cover the palms of both of your hands with tempered chocolate. Pick up a ganache center and roll it in the palms of your hands until thoroughly coated. Set on parchment paper; continue until all centers have been coated. When the first coat is hardened, coat your palms with tempered chocolate again and cover truffles with a second coat. Sprinkle the top with finely chopped peppermint sticks before the chocolate hardens. The wet chocolate will act as glue for the peppermint.

CHAPTER THIRTEEN

Chocolate Gives

DEBORAH'S CHAMBORD TRUFFLE
❧ THE ONE THAT STANDS OUT IN A CROWD ☙

SEMI-SWEET GANACHE CENTER

FLAVORED WITH CHAMBORD LIQUEUR

ROLLED IN WHITE FRENCH CHOCOLATE

SPRINKLED WITH DRIED RED RASPBERRIES

A Chinese proverb says, "To understand a mother's love, bear your own children." Bearing my own children has taught me not only about a mother's love but also how mothers give. It's just what they do. They sacrifice themselves so that their children are cared for. And even when it seems they would have nothing left to give, they give some more.

Looking back, I see so many ways my mother, Deborah, gave to my sisters and me. She started a home-based business so that she could spend the money she earned on special things for her girls— pretty prom dresses, perms for our hair (hey, it was the eighties), and extra spending money. She wanted to give us all the things she didn't have when she was growing up.

Perhaps most important of all, Mom gave me her time. I fondly remember our frequent after-school walks—just the two of us. It was always the same route, up Seventh Avenue, across the park, and back home down Eighth. The trek took about thirty minutes, and I usually talked the whole way—but I don't even remember what I talked about! What mattered most was that I had my mom's undivided attention.

Through the years, friends have come and friends have gone. Yet through the years I've realized that I have had a friend in my mother all along. And, to be honest, the notion is a little awkward.

I mean, the Bible says to honor our father and mother. It's one of the first commandments God gave us. In my house, honoring meant looking up to our parents with respect, not linking arms in side-by-side camaraderie.

Mom took her role as a mother very seriously, and it was important to her that she be a voice of authority rather than a voice of empathy. So goes the mire of conflicting emotions between mothers and daughters . . .

My mother's priority was to raise me "right." And to her, Proverbs 22:6—"Train up a child in the way he should go . . ."—meant hiding her flaws from me in order to perfectly model right living. Very seldom did she let her humanity show. She would never have wanted to give me a wrong impression. I didn't realize that she wasn't trying to be hard on me; I didn't know that her approach was just different.

As I child, I also longed to see my mom's humanity because I knew I could never be as perfect as she was. Furthermore, being an artist by nature, I struggled with black-and-white concepts. Even Old Testament stories were hard for me to grasp: I couldn't understand why God would be so harsh and judgmental. I was too young to sort it all out logically, but I longed to know that grace was real, that mistakes were forgiven, and that my inability to walk the line was somehow covered in it all.

When I was about thirteen, a dear friend of my mother's died unexpectedly. It had to be painful for her, yet my mom did not shed a tear or show any sign of grief, at least not in front of me anyway. That was her modus operandi—to deal with her "weaknesses" privately, before God, rather than impose her feelings on anyone else.

A few weeks after her friend's funeral, my mother gave me the best gift she could have ever given me, a memory of my walk-the-line mother that I will always cherish. It was a moment in time when she, without knowing it, took a brief detour that set my spirit free.

On this particular night, my dad took us all for a long drive out in the country. That was our custom when he and Mom needed to unwind. My sisters and I were "asleep" on the pull-out bed in the back of the van, the front windows were rolled down, and Mom and Dad had been silent for a long time. I was listening to Amy Grant on my headphones and watching the night sky out the window.

That's when it happened. A very taboo sound—at least taboo in my strict, conservative, Christian household—floated my way from the

front of the van. I arched my head up slightly toward the source and couldn't believe what I saw. My mother had her head back against the seat, her bare feet were propped up on the dashboard, and she was listening to the Beatles!

My mother? Listening to the godless rock and roll that was taking America to hell in a handbasket? (That's what I had been told my whole life!) My mother was listening to that kind of music? How could this be? I'd never so much as seen my mother break the speed limit, and all rock and roll was considered sinful in our circles. We weren't even allowed to play the radio in our house! I remember turning my head back toward the night sky, taking my headphones off, closing my eyes, and taking in the cold air and the sound of the music. I had all of these new thoughts—about Mom, about God, about living right, and about grace—to mull over.

When I later learned that Mom's dear friend had been a fan of the Beatles, I realized that the music my mother listened to that night was a tribute to her lost friend. I'd seen my mother grieve in her own way. I'd seen her as a real human being—maybe for the first time. I also saw God that night. And it set me free.

So I wanted my mother's truffle to not only reflect her beauty but also to really stand out when positioned in a display case among all the other flavors. The contrast of the dried red raspberries sprinkled on the swirled white chocolate is a sight to behold. My customers often tell me that it is my prettiest truffle, and I think, *Good, I did my job!* Chambord is a raspberry liqueur, and raspberries are both beautiful and flavorful—just like my mother. Of course, raspberry seeds are hard to deal with, and Mother is, admittedly, a little high maintenance, so the raspberry definitely works! Like she says, "I'm worth it, aren't I?" So every time my mother eats one of "her" truffles, I hope she realizes that I think, yes, she is worth it! ✻

And . . . every man should eat and drink and enjoy the good of all his labor—it is the gift of God. — *Ecclesiastes 3:13*

She gave

I grew

She gave

I learned

She gave

I trusted

She gave

I feared

She gave

I resented

She gave

I questioned

She gave

I matured

She gave

I noticed

Thank you, Mom, for giving yourself to me.

A CHOCOLATE-COVERED
~ CHRISTMAS ~

Chocolate gives us pleasure, satisfaction, elation, comfort, energy, nutrition . . . and the list goes on and on. She is so good at giving that she is a gift in and of herself. We give the gift of chocolate to friends, sisters, mothers, and others as expressions ranging from celebration to sympathy.

Chocolate is such a universally appropriate gift that many corporations even give her as a gift at Christmastime. I can attest to this because I do over half of my annual business during the six weeks before Christmas.

For a chocolatier, that translates into six weeks of sleepless nights, hiring extra staff, meeting stressful deadlines, frequent encounters with delivery trucks, and more packing peanuts and dirty dishes than snowflakes!

It also means missing *A Charlie Brown Christmas* on TV, being absent at good friends' Christmas parties, and, regrettably, not attending the candlelight service at church.

One year, for our family, those six weeks even meant not putting up a Christmas tree until midnight on Christmas Eve. That year we were still living in the loft apartment above our Main Street chocolate shop. My husband and I had closed the shop that night, eaten dinner, and then, as we were tucking the kids into bed, my four-year-old son asked me, "Mommy, is Santa going to bring us a Christmas tree?"

My heart melted into a puddle on the floor. I couldn't believe that I'd let myself put off such an important task. In that moment, I realized I had put my business before my children—something I had vowed I would never do.

Needless to say, after the kids nodded off, I began frantically looking through my closets for our Christmas decorations. They were nowhere to be found. Then it dawned on me: when we moved our family above the chocolate shop, we'd stored a lot of our extra stuff—including the Christmas decorations—in a friend's attic. It was midnight, much too late to retrieve our things. I sat down and cried.

> "What you see before you is the result of a lifetime of chocolate." — *Katharine Hepburn*

Then I remembered the shop's front window. It was full of Christmas decorations!

I put on my slippers and hurried down the stairs to save Christmas. I would have been quite a sight to any passersby. I was standing in my pajamas in the lighted window taking down the Christmas tree. Ornaments were wobbling and lights dangling. I imagined the conversation I'd have with police officers should they come knocking, mistaking me for a modern-day Grinch.

When my husband saw me, he just smiled and shook his head like he does when he catches me in the middle of some harebrained plan. He helped me finagle the awkward mass around the corner, and within ten minutes we had a glimmering tree waiting to be adored by wide-eyed children on Christmas morning.

I realized that I could've sunk into a quicksand trap of my failures. After all, what kind of mother forgets the Christmas tree? But, as I stood in the shadow of the tree and straightened a few strands of lights, my fingers stumbled upon a familiar substance—chocolate. Apparently, as I'd traipsed through the shop with lights dragging behind me, they'd encountered chocolate.

And God once again used the gift of chocolate to remind me that He's got it all covered. ✻

Peppermint Bark Recipe

YOU WILL NEED

1 pound white chocolate, divided

1 pound dark chocolate, divided

2 cups crushed peppermint sticks

MELT ⅔ OF THE POUND OF DARK CHOCOLATE in a double boiler, stirring constantly. Use the remaining ⅓ of the pound for tempering (see tempering instructions on pages 18 and 19).

Using an offset spatula (a long metal spatula with a stiff blade that bends up where it meets the handle), spread the dark chocolate out on parchment paper to ⅛-inch thickness. Let it rest until it is dry to the touch.

Melt ⅔ of the pound of white chocolate in a double boiler. Use the remaining ⅓ of the pound for tempering.

Using the offset spatula, spread the white chocolate out on the dark chocolate slab to ⅛-inch thickness. Immediately sprinkle the 2 cups crushed peppermint evenly over the entire surface of the white chocolate layer. Let the peppermint bark rest until the chocolate is dry to the touch.

By hand, break the bark into random-sized pieces, approximately 2 x 2 inches in size. Store in a sealed container at room temperature for up to 6 weeks until ready to serve.

Bethany Thouin

Bethany Thouin is an artisan chocolatier who for five years served people from her chocolate café in historic Franklin, Tennessee. Customers and recipients of her signature truffles include Faith Hill, LeAnn Rimes, Nicole Kidman, Ashley Judd, Wolfgang Puck, and President Bush. Named one of the Top 10 Rising Stars in American Chocolate in 2004, she has appeared on the *Food Network Challenge* and has presented a chocolate dress designed by her eldest daughter in the New York City Chocolate Show. She and her husband Jesse have four children. You can visit her website at www.bethanychocolatier.com.

Angela Fox

Angela Folds Fox is a wife, mother, writer, and lover of all things creative . . . and all things covered with chocolate! She is the founder of www.creativedaycafe.com, a resource offering creative inspiration to artists and creative-hopefuls. As a freelance writer her articles have appeared in *Christian Retailing*, *Giftware News*, *Inspirational Giftware*, and various Christian publications. She also writes a weekly newspaper column in the *Franklin Review Appeal* and is putting the finishing touches on her first novel. Angela, her husband Jerry and son, Brayden, reside in Franklin, Tennessee.